BASIC/NOT BORING

MATH COMPUTATION & PROBLEM SOLVING

Grades 2-3

Inventive Exercises to Sharpen Skills and Raise Achievement

Series Concept & Development
by Imogene Forte & Marjorie Frank
Exercises by Marjorie Frank

Incentive Publications, Inc.
Nashville, Tennessee

Thanks to Maurine Bridges for her assistance

About the cover:
> Bound resist, or tie dye, is the most ancient known method of
> fabric surface design. The brilliance of the basic tie dye design
> on this cover reflects the possibilities that emerge from the
> mastery of basic skills.

Illustrated by Kathleen Bullock
Cover art by Mary Patricia Deprez, dba Tye Dye Mary®
Cover design by Marta Drayton, Joe Shibley, and W. Paul Nance
Edited by Anna Quinn

ISBN 0-86530-394-0

TABLE OF CONTENTS

Appendix

CELEBRATE BASIC MATH SKILLS

Basic does not mean boring! There is certainly nothing dull about . . .
　. . . tracking down mysterious forces and hidden machines
　. . . following a snorkeler to count underwater creatures
　. . . figuring out who wins a frog race, a bug race, or a boat race
　. . . using numbers to get down a wild river in a raft
　. . . tracking down missing numbers in hideouts and caves
　. . . finding the identity of a mystery athlete
　. . . solving problems with hula hoops, pizzas, and
　　　snowballs

The idea of celebrating the basics is just what it sounds like—enjoying and improving the skills of using numbers and solving problems. Each page of this book invites young learners to try a high-interest, visually appealing exercise that will sharpen one specific content skill. This is not just any ordinary fill-in-the-blanks way to learn. These exercises are fun and surprising, and they make good use of thinking skills. Students will do the useful work of practicing math skills while they enjoy exciting adventures with numbers and solve sports-related problems.

The pages in this book can be used in many ways:
- to review or practice a math skill with one student
- to sharpen the skill with a small or large group
- to start off a lesson on a particular skill
- to assess how well a student has mastered a skill

Each page has directions that are written simply. It is intended that an adult be available to help students read the information on the page, if help is needed. In most cases, the pages will best be used as a follow-up to a lesson or concept which has been taught. The pages are excellent tools for immediate reinforcement of a concept.

As your students take on the challenges of these adventures with math, they will grow! And as you watch them check off the basic math skills they've acquired or strengthened, you can celebrate with them.

The Skills Test

Use the skills test beginning on page 57 as a pretest and/or a post-test. This will help you check the students' mastery of basic computation and problem-solving skills and prepare them for success on achievement tests.

SKILLS CHECKLIST
MATH COMPUTATION & PROBLEM SOLVING, GRADES 2-3

✔	SKILL	PAGE(S)
	Compare and order whole numbers	10, 13, 15-17
	Identify odd and even numbers	11
	Work with ordinals	12
	Read and write whole numbers	14, 15, 18-20
	Identify patterns in groups of numbers	15
	Identify place value to 6 places	18, 19
	Round numbers to the nearest place	20
	Use addition facts to 20; identify fact families	21
	Use subtraction facts to 20; identify fact families	21
	Add whole numbers with and without renaming	22, 23, 26, 27, 33, 36
	Add columns of 3 or more addends	23
	Subtract whole numbers with and without renaming	24-27, 33, 36
	Check accuracy of answers	26
	Skip count	29
	Use multiplication/division facts for 1-10; identify fact families	28-31
	Use multiplication for computations	30, 33
	Do simple division computations	31-33
	Find missing numbers in simple equations	34
	Use estimation and mental math to make computations	33, 36
	Choose the correct operation for a problem	35, 50-53
	Read and write fractions	37-42
	Identify and write mixed numerals	39
	Add and subtract fractions with like denominators	40
	Read, write, and order decimals	42, 43
	Write fractions (with tenths) as decimals	42
	Identify some equivalent fractions	41
	Complete a variety of time-telling tasks; work with dates	44-48
	Write, compare, and estimate amounts of money	49-52
	Count money	49
	Solve problems with money	49-52
	Solve problems using maps, charts, and tables	44-48
	Solve problems using illustrations	16, 17, 34-39, 41-43, 50
	Solve word problems, including multi-step problems	46, 50, 51, 53

MATH COMPUTATION & PROBLEM SOLVING
Grades 2-3

Skills Exercises

The Big Race

These rowers are in a big race. Who is racing against them?
Follow the dots to find out.

Start with number 67. Connect the dots from the smallest to the largest number shown.

Color the picture!

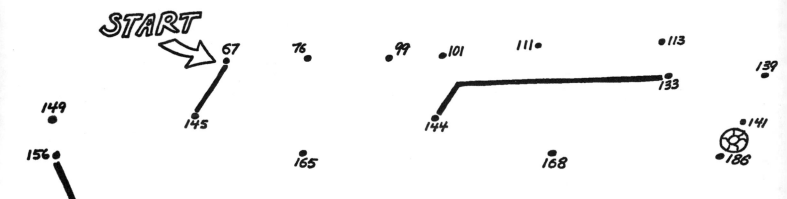

Name _____

Number Search

Numbers are everywhere in this picture!
Some are odd. Some are even.
Color all the **even** numbers in red.
How many did you find? _____
Color all the **odd** numbers in green.
How many did you find? _____

An **even** number is a number with
0, 2, 4, 6, or 8 in the one's place.
An **odd** number is a number with
1, 3, 5, 7, or 9 in the one's place.

Name _____

Meet the Athletes

Here are some of the athletes in Benjy's neighborhood.
Read the name, age, and sport of each one.
Then answer the questions about the order they are in
from left to right.

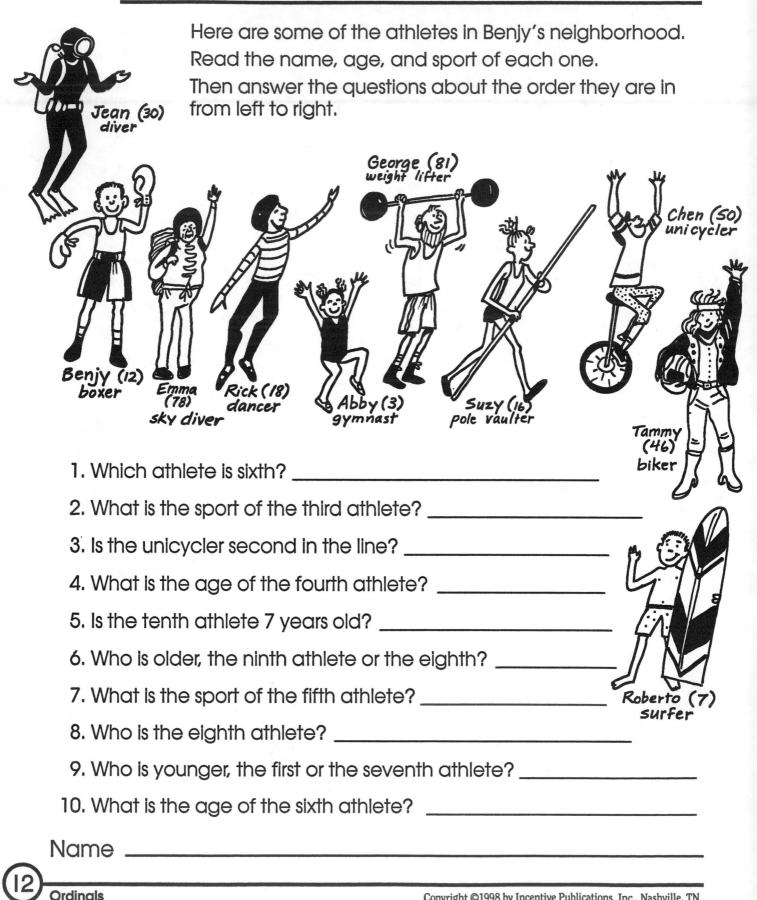

1. Which athlete is sixth? _____

2. What is the sport of the third athlete? _____

3. Is the unicycler second in the line? _____

4. What is the age of the fourth athlete? _____

5. Is the tenth athlete 7 years old? _____

6. Who is older, the ninth athlete or the eighth? _____

7. What is the sport of the fifth athlete? _____

8. Who is the eighth athlete? _____

9. Who is younger, the first or the seventh athlete? _____

10. What is the age of the sixth athlete? _____

Name _____

Numbers Dropping from the Sky

The sky is filled with numbers! Each parachute has one.
Find the numbers to match the number words written below.
Color each parachute as the chart shows.

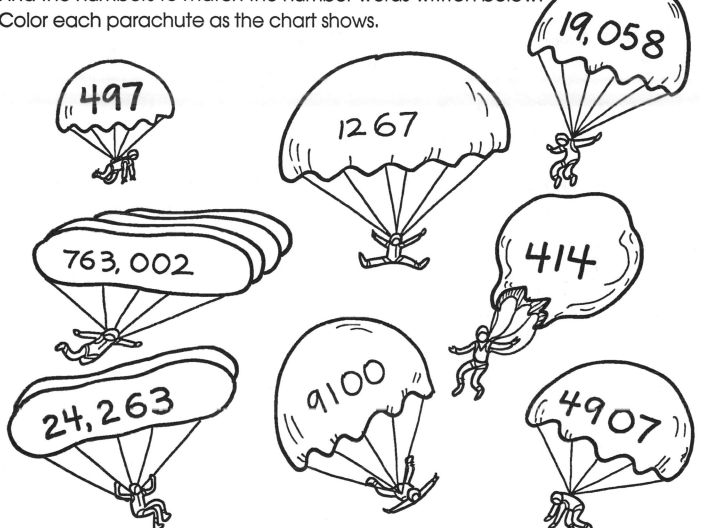

	Number	Color
1	seven hundred sixty-three thousand, two	blue
2	four hundred ninety-seven	pink spots
3	nineteen thousand, fifty-eight	green stripes
4	four hundred fourteen	red stripes
5	twenty-four thousand, two hundred sixty-three	black & purple
6	nine thousand, one hundred	yellow
7	four thousand, nine hundred, seven	orange
8	one thousand, two hundred, sixty-seven	blue & green

Name _____

Reading Whole Numbers

A Whole Lot of Bouncing Going On!

22 kids have taken turns on Jana's trampoline.
The numbers in the puzzle tell how many
times each one has bounced.
Read the clues that give the number words.
Write the numbers into the puzzle.

CLUES

Down

1. two hundred sixty-two
2. one thousand
3. nine thousand, one hundred, thirty
4. seven hundred sixteen
6. nineteen
9. three hundred twelve
10. four hundred twenty-one
11. two hundred ninety-five
12. nine hundred three
13. two hundred eighty-six
15. seventeen

Across

1. twenty-nine
4. seven thousand
5. two hundred eleven
7. thirty
8. ninety-six
9. three hundred four
11. twenty
13. twenty-two
14. fifty-one
16. eighty-eight
17. thirty-nine

Name _____

Copyright ©1998 by Incentive Publications, Inc., Nashville, TN.

Basic Skills/Math 2-3

Patterns on the Bench

Some members of the softball team are waiting on the bench.
The numbers on their shirts follow a pattern.

| The pattern is +3 to each shirt. The next number will be 24. |

Fill in the missing numbers for each row of shirts.

1. 2 4 8 ___ 32 64

2. 3 7 ___ 15 ___

3. 15 11 ___ 3

4. 2 3 5 8 ___

5. 9 ___ 7 6 ___

Name _____

Underwater Search

Snorkeler Sam is counting things under the sea.
Follow the directions at the bottom of the page for coloring the picture.
Use the picture to solve the problems on the next page (page 17).

Color the sharks purple.   Color the turtles green.
Color the small fish yellow.   Color each octopus gray.
Color the seahorse orange.   Color the treasure chests brown.
Color the crabs red.   Color the shells pink.

Name _____

Comparing Whole Numbers

Underwater Search, continued . . .

Compare the numbers of things
in the picture on page 16.
Put >, <, or = in each box below.

> means greater than
< means less than
= means equal to

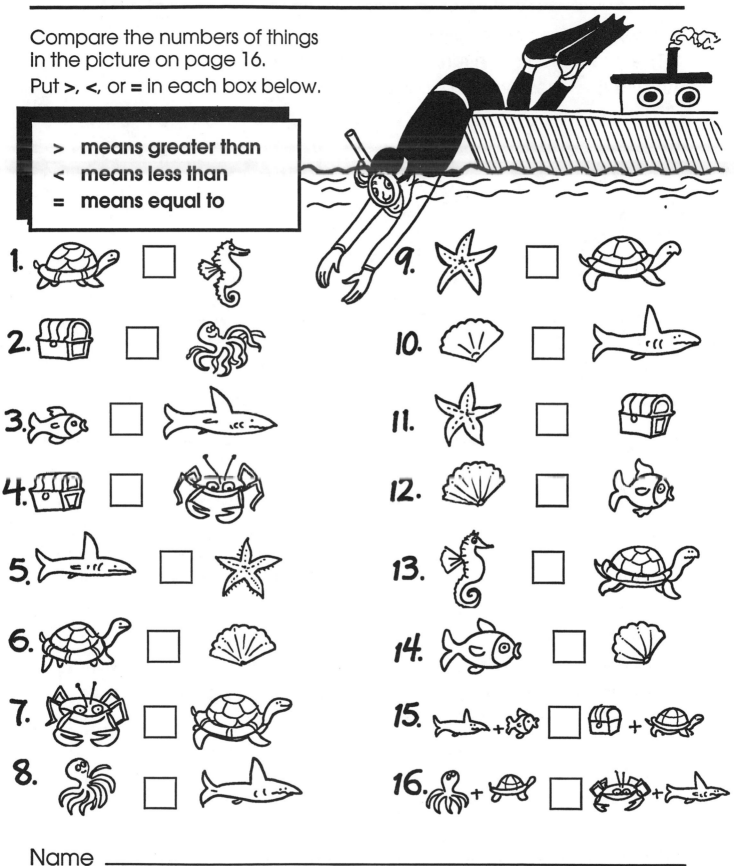

1. 🐢 ☐ 🌊
2. 📦 ☐ 🐙
3. 🐟 ☐ 🦈
4. 📦 ☐ 🦀
5. 🦈 ☐ ⭐
6. 🐢 ☐ 🐚
7. 🦀 ☐ 🐢
8. 🐙 ☐ 🦈

9. ⭐ ☐ 🐢
10. 🐚 ☐ 🦈
11. ⭐ ☐ 📦
12. 🐚 ☐ 🐟
13. 🌊 ☐ 🐢
14. 🐟 ☐ 🐚
15. 🦈 + 🐟 ☐ 📦 + 🐢
16. 🐙 + 🐢 ☐ 🦀 + 🦈

Name _____

Use with page 16.
(17)

Comparing Whole Numbers
Basic Skills/Math 2-3

The Great Bug Race

Every year these bugs run a big race.
While you watch them run, look at the numbers on their shirts.
Answer the questions below about place value.

1. Color the body of the bug with 6 in the hundreds place purple.
2. Color the body of the bug with 5 in the thousands place green.
3. Put red spots on the bug with the 0 in the tens place.
4. Put yellow stripes on the bug with the 4 in the ones place.
5. Color the bug with 3 in the hundred thousands place brown.
6. Draw feelers on the bug with the 4 in the ten thousands place.
7. Color the bug with 3 in the tens place orange.
8. Find the bug with the 0 in the ones place. Color it black.
9. Color the shoes red on the bug with the 4 in the hundreds place.
10. Find the bug with the 7 in the ones place. Color her shoes yellow.

Name _____

Place Value

Which Number Am I?

Athletes wear many different kinds of footwear.
Each of these pieces of footwear has a question for you.
The answer is the number described by the clues. Write each number.

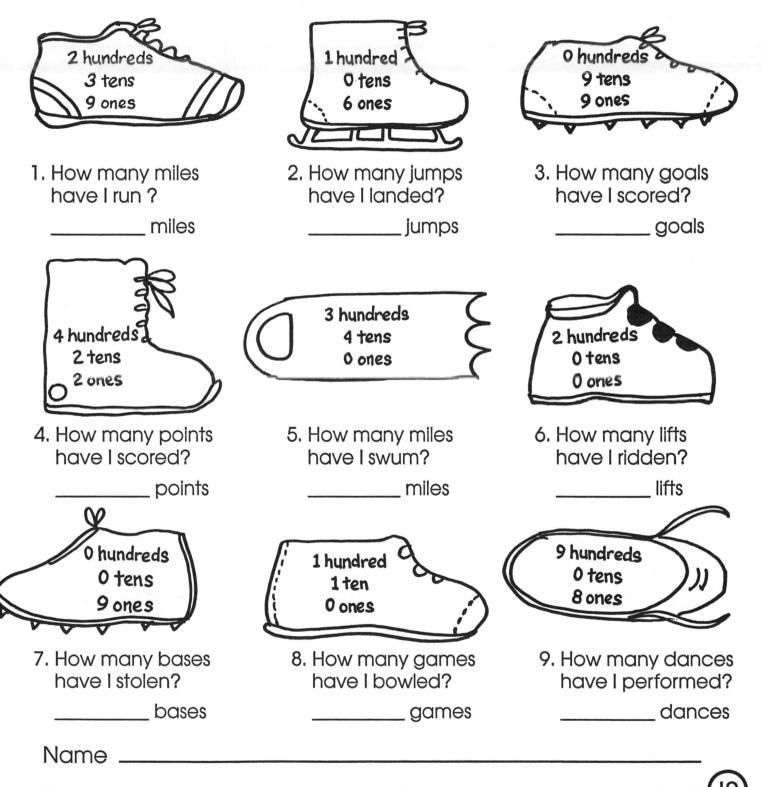

2 hundreds
3 tens
9 ones

1. How many miles
   have I run ?

_____ miles

1 hundred
0 tens
6 ones

2. How many jumps
   have I landed?

_____ jumps

0 hundreds
9 tens
9 ones

3. How many goals
   have I scored?

_____ goals

4 hundreds
2 tens
2 ones

4. How many points
   have I scored?

_____ points

3 hundreds
4 tens
0 ones

5. How many miles
   have I swum?

_____ miles

2 hundreds
0 tens
0 ones

6. How many lifts
   have I ridden?

_____ lifts

0 hundreds
0 tens
9 ones

7. How many bases
   have I stolen?

_____ bases

1 hundred
1 ten
0 ones

8. How many games
   have I bowled?

_____ games

9 hundreds
0 tens
8 ones

9. How many dances
   have I performed?

_____ dances

Name _____

Place Value

Join the Round-up!

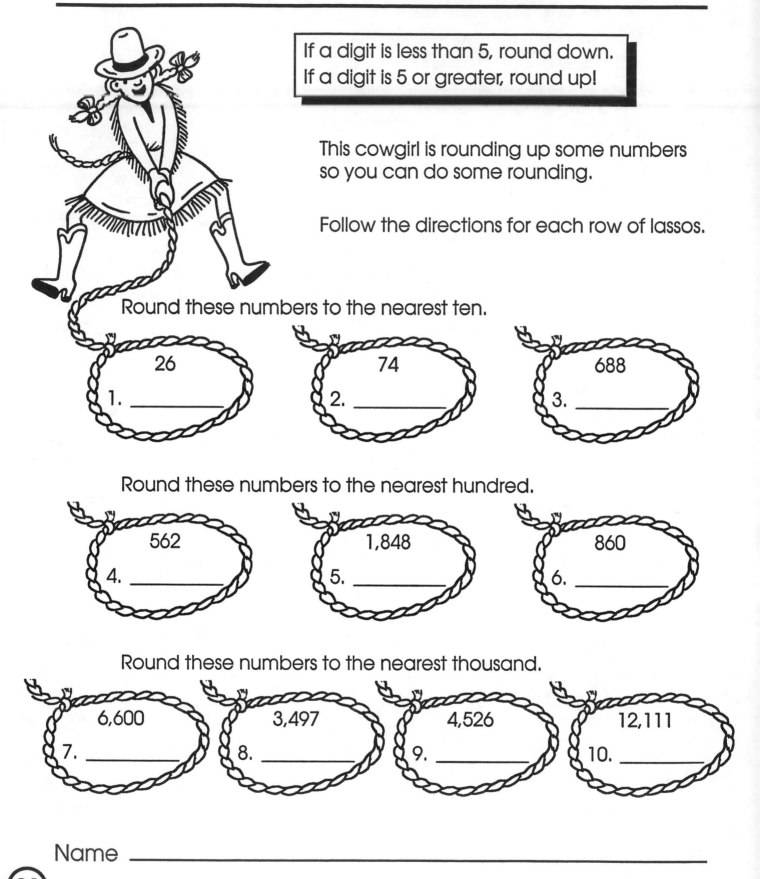

If a digit is less than 5, round down.
If a digit is 5 or greater, round up!

This cowgirl is rounding up some numbers so you can do some rounding.

Follow the directions for each row of lassos.

Round these numbers to the nearest ten.

26
1. _____

74
2. _____

688
3. _____

Round these numbers to the nearest hundred.

562
4. _____

1,848
5. _____

860
6. _____

Round these numbers to the nearest thousand.

6,600
7. _____

3,497
8. _____

4,526
9. _____

12,111
10. _____

Name _____

Sports Runs in the Family

READY... AIM..., SMILE!

The Morris family is a family of sports lovers.
The problems below each show
a fact family.

Addition and subtraction facts
come in families.

8, 7, and 15 are all in
a family because

$8 + 7 = 15$ $7 + 8 = 15$

$15 - 7 = 8$ $15 - 8 = 7$

Fill in the missing fact in each of these families.

1) $12 - 6 = \boxed{}$

   $\boxed{} + 6 = 12$

2) $2 + \boxed{} = 9$

   $9 - \boxed{} = 2$

3) $3 + \boxed{} = 7$

   $7 - 3 = \boxed{}$

4) $6 + \boxed{} = 10$

   $10 - 6 = \boxed{}$

5) $\boxed{} + 2 = 10$

   $10 - 2 = \boxed{}$

6) $9 - \boxed{} = 5$

   $5 + \boxed{} = 9$

7) $7 - 5 = \boxed{}$

   $7 - \boxed{} = 5$

8) $9 - 6 = \boxed{}$

   $6 + \boxed{} = 9$

9) $9 + \boxed{} = 17$

   $17 - 9 = \boxed{}$

Name _____

Lost in the Weeds

Michael has lost his sports equipment in the weeds. What is it?
Solve each addition problem. Find the answer in the code box.
Color each section with the color that matches the answer.

Code

36 = blue	84 = yellow
99 = green	62 = orange
70 = brown	100 = red
179 = purple	

Name _____

Throw Three!

In this dart game, Ramon gets to throw 3 darts in each game.
Add up his score for each game.
Which game is his best?

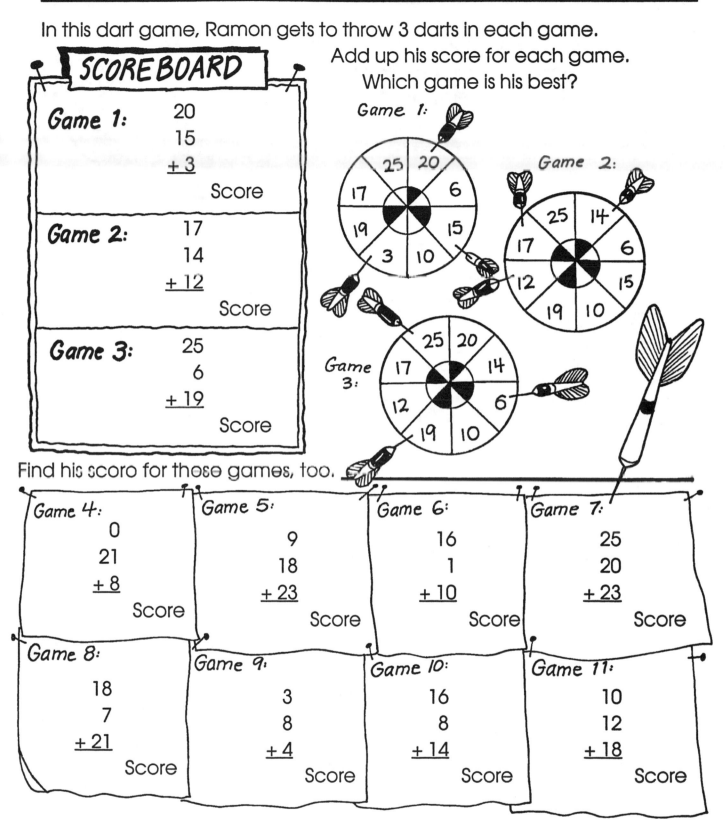

SCOREBOARD

Game 1:
20
15
+ 3
_____
Score

Game 2:
17
14
+ 12
_____
Score

Game 3:
25
6
+ 19
_____
Score

Game 1:

Game 2:

Game 3:

Find his score for these games, too.

Game 4:
0
21
+ 8
_____
Score

Game 5:
9
18
+ 23
_____
Score

Game 6:
16
1
+ 10
_____
Score

Game 7:
25
20
+ 23
_____
Score

Game 8:
18
7
+ 21
_____
Score

Game 9:
3
8
+ 4
_____
Score

Game 10:
16
8
+ 14
_____
Score

Game 11:
10
12
+ 18
_____
Score

Name _____

Column Addition

Different Sails

A **difference** is the answer in a subtraction problem.

Each sail has a different difference!
Solve the subtraction problems on each sail.
Then follow the directions for coloring the sails
in the box at the bottom.

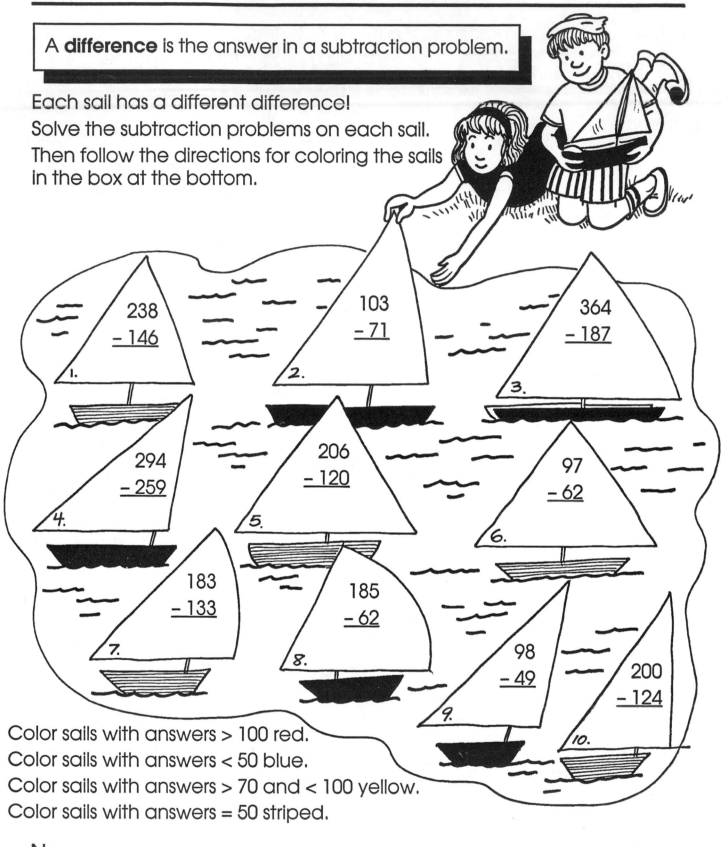

1. 238
   − 146

2. 103
   − 71

3. 364
   − 187

4. 294
   − 259

5. 206
   − 120

6. 97
   − 62

7. 183
   − 133

8. 185
   − 62

9. 98
   − 49

10. 200
    − 124

Color sails with answers > 100 red.
Color sails with answers < 50 blue.
Color sails with answers > 70 and < 100 yellow.
Color sails with answers = 50 striped.

Name _____

Subtracting Snowballs

Every time one of the teams throws a snowball, they have to subtract it from their stack.

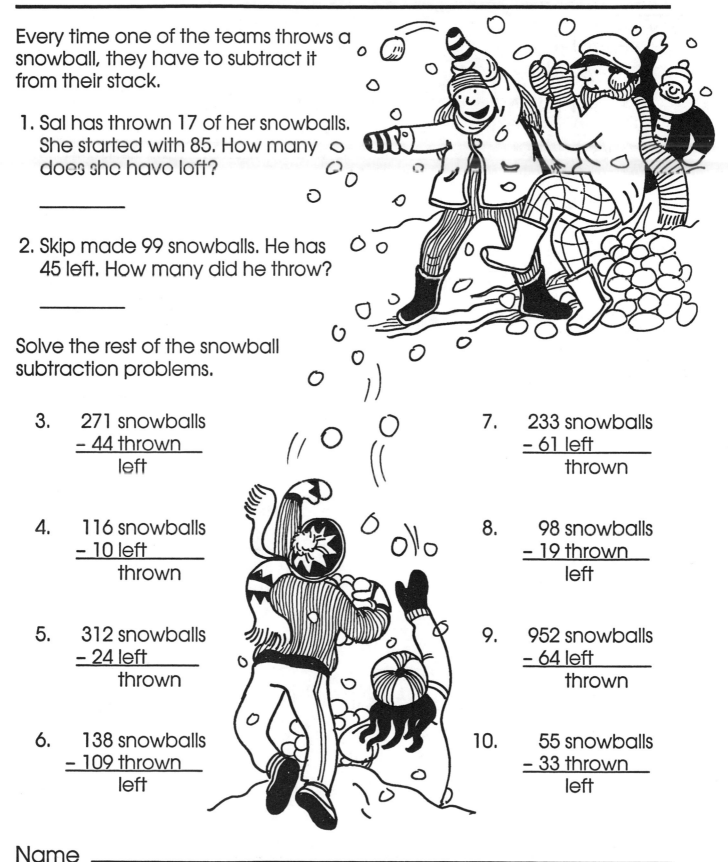

1. Sal has thrown 17 of her snowballs. She started with 85. How many does she have left?

   _____

2. Skip made 99 snowballs. He has 45 left. How many did he throw?

   _____

Solve the rest of the snowball subtraction problems.

3. 271 snowballs
    – 44 thrown
        left

4. 116 snowballs
    – 10 left
        thrown

5. 312 snowballs
    – 24 left
        thrown

6. 138 snowballs
    – 109 thrown
        left

7. 233 snowballs
    – 61 left
        thrown

8. 98 snowballs
    – 19 thrown
        left

9. 952 snowballs
    – 64 left
        thrown

10. 55 snowballs
    – 33 thrown
        left

Name _____

Homework at the Gym

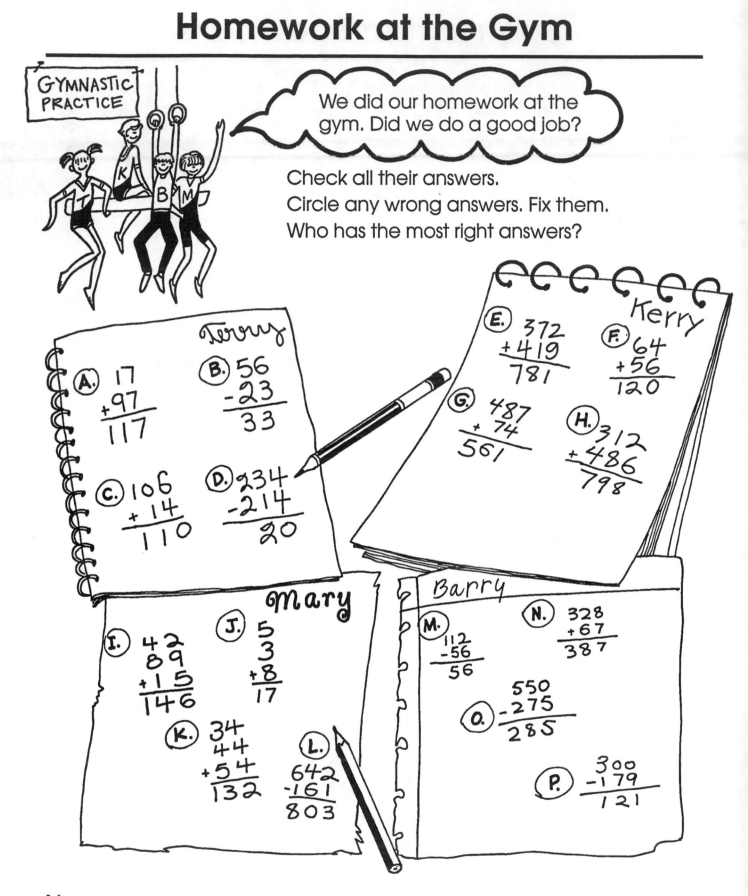

GYMNASTIC PRACTICE

We did our homework at the gym. Did we do a good job?

Check all their answers.
Circle any wrong answers. Fix them.
Who has the most right answers?

Terry

A.
17
+97
117

B.
56
-23
33

C.
106
+14
110

D.
234
-214
20

Kerry

E.
372
+419
781

F.
64
+56
120

G.
487
+74
561

H.
312
+486
798

Mary

I.
42
89
+15
146

J.
5
3
+8
17

K.
34
44
+54
132

L.
642
-161
803

Barry

M.
112
-56
56

N.
328
+67
387

O.
550
-275
285

P.
300
-179
121

Name _____

Addition & Subtraction • Accuracy

Surprising Sports Facts

When you solve these problems, you will get answers to some interesting sports facts. You might already know some of these facts. Others might surprise you!

1.   71
   − 49

feet on a starting soccer team

2.   48
   − 39

Olympic gold medals held by U.S. swimmer Mark Spitz

3.   99
   − 74

age of the youngest world champion race-car driver

4. 1340
  +1151

points scored by Michael Jordan in 1995-1996 season

5.   123
   −109

age of the youngest women's world champion figure skater

6.   11
   + 15

miles in a marathon

7.   760
   − 755

rings in the Olympic symbol

8.   259
   −243

balls in a billiard (pool) game

9.   156
   + 144

yards in the length of a polo field

10. 850
   − 829

points in a ping-pong match

11.   39
   + 15

outs in a 9-inning baseball game

12.   92
   − 88

riders in an Olympic bobsled

13. 263
   + 137

dimples on a golf ball

Name _____

Noises in the Woods

The campers are hearing sounds in the woods.
What things might be hiding in the woods around them?
You'll find out when you solve the problems.
Follow the color code to color the puzzle pieces.
(Some things might be upside-down!)

Color Code
6, 30, 5 = black
7, 48, 49, 9 = green
24 = orange
8, 28 = brown
3, 36 = yellow
4 = pink

Name _____

Multiplication & Division Facts

Who Wins the Race?

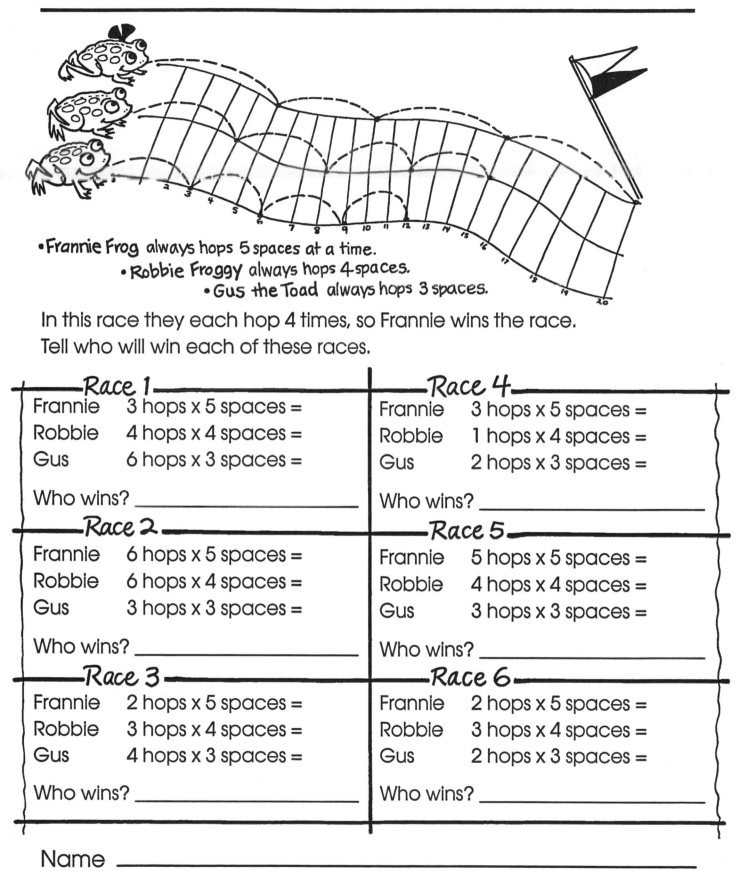

- Frannie Frog always hops 5 spaces at a time.
- Robbie Froggy always hops 4 spaces.
- Gus the Toad always hops 3 spaces.

In this race they each hop 4 times, so Frannie wins the race.

Tell who will win each of these races.

Race 1

Frannie   3 hops x 5 spaces =

Robbie   4 hops x 4 spaces =

Gus   6 hops x 3 spaces =

Who wins? _____

Race 2

Frannie   6 hops x 5 spaces =

Robbie   6 hops x 4 spaces =

Gus   3 hops x 3 spaces =

Who wins? _____

Race 3

Frannie   2 hops x 5 spaces =

Robbie   3 hops x 4 spaces =

Gus   4 hops x 3 spaces =

Who wins? _____

Race 4

Frannie   3 hops x 5 spaces =

Robbie   1 hops x 4 spaces =

Gus   2 hops x 3 spaces =

Who wins? _____

Race 5

Frannie   5 hops x 5 spaces =

Robbie   4 hops x 4 spaces =

Gus   3 hops x 3 spaces =

Who wins? _____

Race 6

Frannie   2 hops x 5 spaces =

Robbie   3 hops x 4 spaces =

Gus   2 hops x 3 spaces =

Who wins? _____

Name _____

Mystery Athlete

Who is the mystery athlete? Solve the problems to find out!
Use the Key to find the letters that match each answer.
Write the letters in the spaces at the bottom of the page.

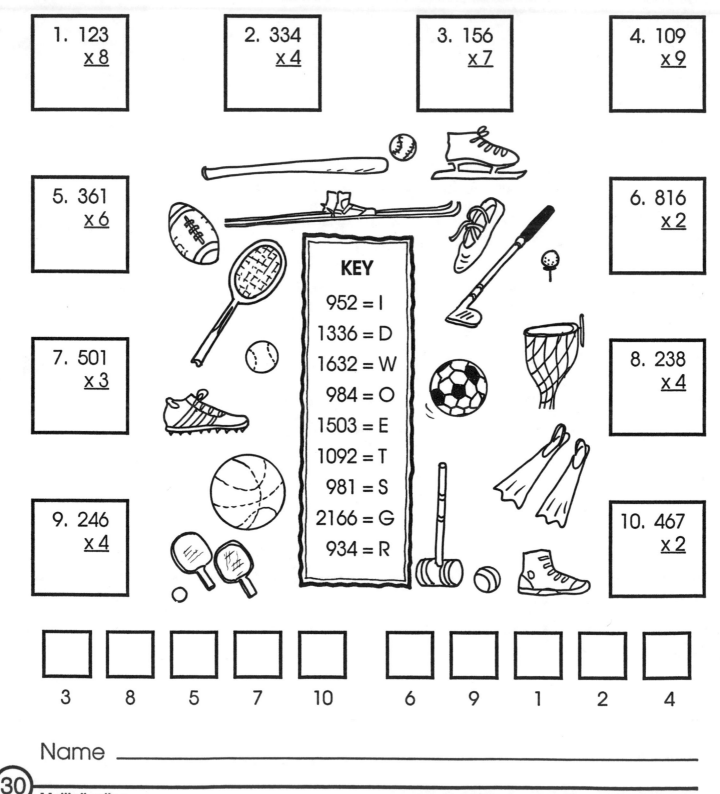

1. 123
   x 8

2. 334
   x 4

3. 156
   x 7

4. 109
   x 9

5. 361
   x 6

6. 816
   x 2

7. 501
   x 3

8. 238
   x 4

9. 246
   x 4

10. 467
    x 2

KEY

952 = I
1336 = D
1632 = W
984 = O
1503 = E
1092 = T
981 = S
2166 = G
934 = R

| 3 | 8 | 5 | 7 | 10 | 6 | 9 | 1 | 2 | 4 |

Name _____

How Many Jumps?

This hurdler jumps 9 spaces with each jump.

He starts at the beginning of the number line and finishes 45 spaces later at the finish line.

He must jump 5 times to get the end.

> We can write this problem.
> 45 spaces ÷ 5 jumps = 9 spaces per jump

Practice these facts.

1. 56 ÷ 7 = ☐ per jump

2. 72 ÷ 8 jumps = ☐ per jump

3. ☐ ÷ 3 jumps = 9 per jump

4. ☐ ÷ 4 jumps = 4 per jump

5. 81 ÷ ☐ jumps = 9 per jump

6. 40 ÷ ☐ jumps = 5 per jump

7. 20 ÷ 5 jumps = ☐ per jump

8. 27 ÷ 3 jumps = ☐ per jump

9. 64 ÷ ☐ jumps = 8 per jump

10. 15 ÷ ☐ jumps = 3 per jump

11. ☐ ÷ 3 jumps = 4 per jump

12. ☐ ÷ 7 jumps = 7 per jump

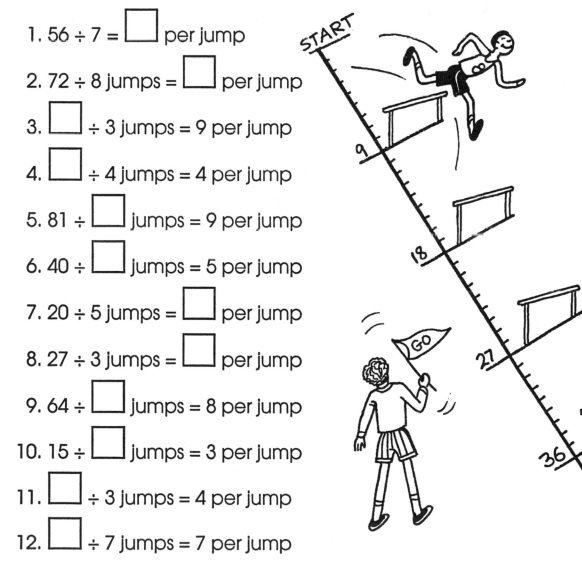

Name _____

Is It Tic Tac Toe?

In each row across, one answer is different from the others.

Put a big, red **X** on the different answer.

To win, you must get a line of X's either across, up and down, or diagonally.

A.

2⟌24	6⟌72	9⟌99
8⟌72	4⟌52	4⟌36
7⟌91	3⟌42	8⟌112

Which games are winners? _____

Ladies and Gentlemen! It's 'Tic-Tac-Toe' by a nose!

B.

4⟌24	6⟌66	9⟌54
2⟌44	7⟌49	3⟌66
7⟌84	5⟌20	4⟌48

C.

8⟌160	5⟌80	7⟌112
9⟌108	4⟌72	7⟌126
8⟌72	7⟌98	9⟌81

Name _____

Wild River Ride

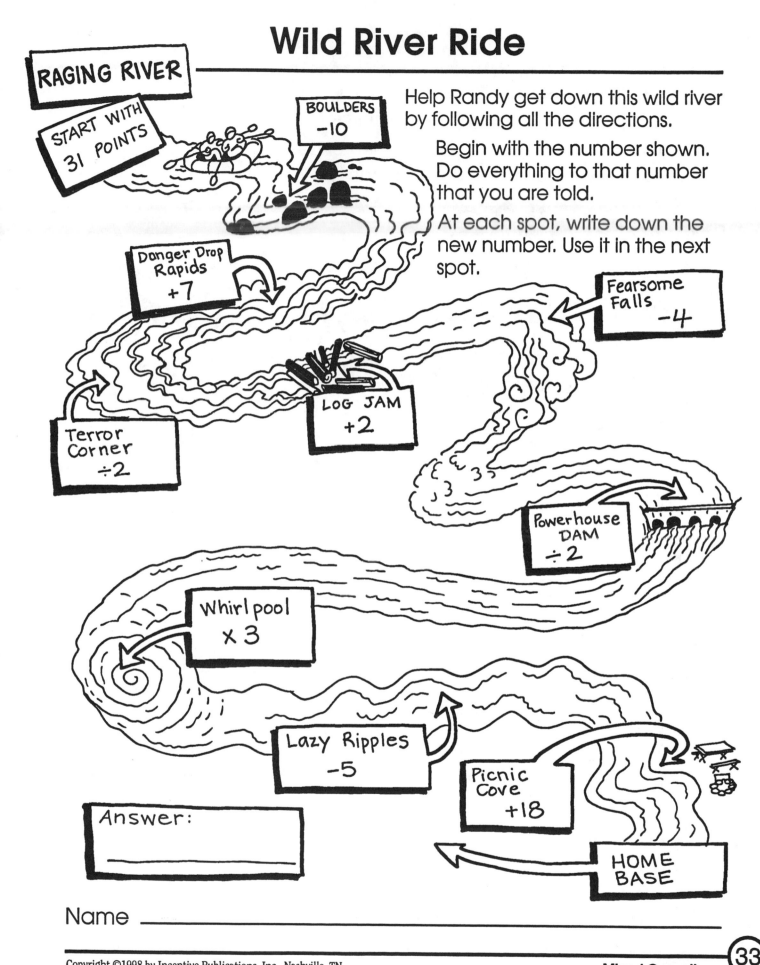

RAGING RIVER

BOULDERS
−10

START WITH
31 POINTS

Help Randy get down this wild river by following all the directions.

Begin with the number shown. Do everything to that number that you are told.

At each spot, write down the new number. Use it in the next spot.

Danger Drop Rapids
+7

Fearsome Falls
−4

Terror Corner
÷2

Log Jam
+2

Powerhouse DAM
÷2

Whirlpool
×3

Lazy Ripples
−5

Picnic Cove
+18

Answer:

HOME BASE

Name

Mixed Operations

Hide & Seek

Chester is playing hide & seek, and he is IT.
Help him find the numbers that are hiding.
Find the number for each number sentence. Put it in the box.
You can use a number more than once.

1) $\square + 10 = 14$

2) $6 \div \square = 3$

3) $\square \times 3 = 21$

4) $9 - \square = 4$

5) $5 + \square = 11$

6) $4 + \square = 11$

7) $2 \times 5 = \square$

8) $24 \div 4 = \square$

9) $8 - \square = 0$

10) $9 \times 2 = \square$

11) $6 + \square = 12$

12) $\square \div 4 = 2$

13) $5 \times 5 = \square$

14) $8 \times \square = 8$

15) $\square - 6 = 3$

16) $\square + 5 = 13$

Name _____

Lost in the Cave

A spelunker is someone who explores caves.

These spelunkers are looking for lost signs to put into the number sentences. Find the right sign for each sentence. Each sign can be used many times.

1. 4 ☐ 7 = 11
2. 3 ☐ 2 = 6
3. 8 ☐ 5 = 3
4. 5 ☐ 3 = 15
5. 6 ☐ 2 = 3

11. 9 ☐ 1 = 9
12. 10 ☐ 2 = 5
13. 5 ☐ 3 = 8
14. 9 ☐ 3 = 3
15. 3 ☐ 3 = 9

6. 4 ☐ 4 = 0
7. 3 ☐ 8 = 24
8. 7 ☐ 2 = 9
9. 14 ☐ 2 = 7
10. 9 ☐ 1 = 10

16. 2 ☐ 6 = 8
17. 5 ☐ 3 = 2
18. 2 ☐ 2 = 4
19. 6 ☐ 6 = 1
20. 10 ☐ 5 = 15

Name _____

Signs for Operations

Which Route?

Help these cross-country runners decide which route to take.

Choose four different colors of crayons or markers. Draw a route for each runner to one of the finish flags. Use a different color for each route.

Add and subtract in your head as you follow each route. Start with the number 8 for each number. Write the number you have at the end of each route.

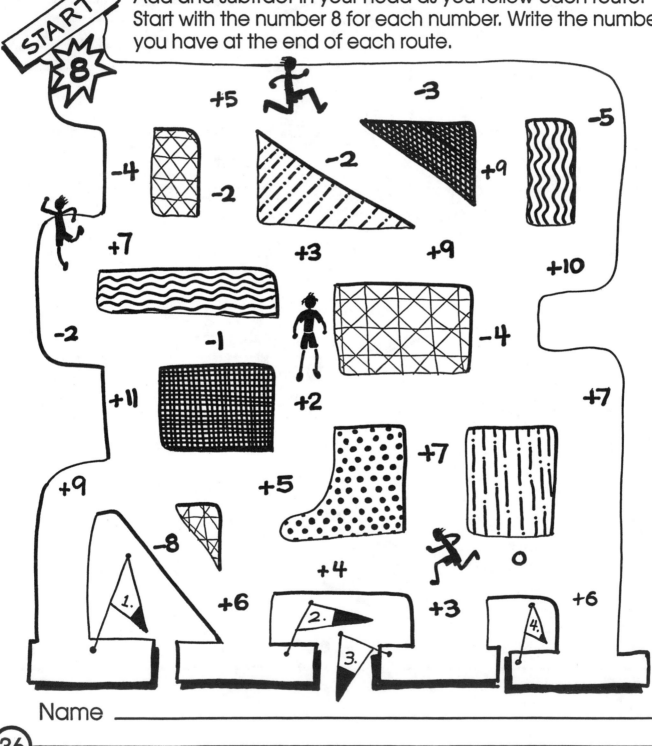

START
8

+5   -3   -5
-4   -2   -2   +9
+7   +3   +9   +10
-2   -1   -4   +7
+11   +2
+9   +5   +7   0
-8   +4   +3   +6
1.   +6   2.   3.   4.

Name _____

Frisbee™ Fractions

Which Frisbee™ is which?
Write the letter to tell which Frisbee™
matches each description.

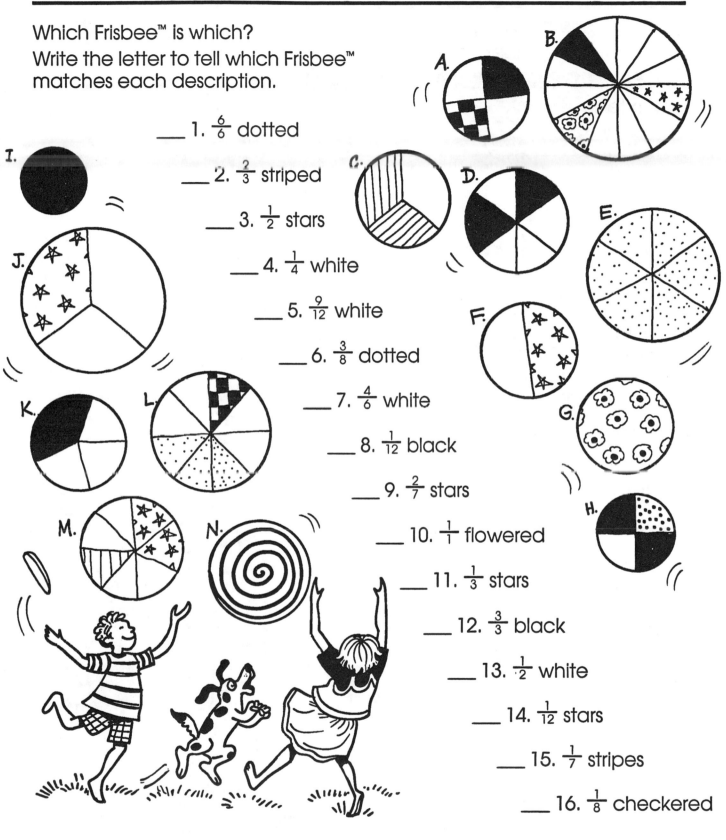

___ 1. $\frac{6}{6}$ dotted

___ 2. $\frac{2}{3}$ striped

___ 3. $\frac{1}{2}$ stars

___ 4. $\frac{1}{4}$ white

___ 5. $\frac{9}{12}$ white

___ 6. $\frac{3}{8}$ dotted

___ 7. $\frac{4}{6}$ white

___ 8. $\frac{1}{12}$ black

___ 9. $\frac{2}{7}$ stars

___ 10. $\frac{1}{1}$ flowered

___ 11. $\frac{1}{3}$ stars

___ 12. $\frac{3}{3}$ black

___ 13. $\frac{1}{2}$ white

___ 14. $\frac{1}{12}$ stars

___ 15. $\frac{1}{7}$ stripes

___ 16. $\frac{1}{8}$ checkered

Name _____

Swimmers Line-up

The top number is the **numerator.** It answers the question.
The bottom number is the **denominator.** It tells how many in all.

The swim team is ready for the big race. Let's take a look at all their equipment!

$\frac{6}{6}$ of the team is ready to go!

Write a fraction to answer each question.

1. How many swimmers have goggles?

2. How many feet have on fins?

3. How many swimmers are wearing suits with stripes?

4. How many swimmers are still wet?

5. How many swimmers are wearing bathing caps?

6. How many feet have aqua socks?

7. How many swimmers are wearing a float?

8. How many swimmers have suits with NO dots?

9. How many noses have a nose plug?

10. How many swimmers have black suits?

Name _____

Pizza Party

A **mixed numeral** is a number that shows a whole number and a fraction.

The football players were really hungry after their games.
They all ate a lot of pizza. Who ate the most?
Write mixed numerals to show how much each player ate.

Rocky ate _____   Ernest ate _____   Bruiser ate _____

Jess ate _____   Kujo ate _____   Bud ate _____

Who ate the most? _____   Who left the most? _____

Name _____

Mixed Numerals

Skateboard Tricks

Adding and subtracting fractions is as easy as riding a skateboard!
You just need to know the trick. When the denominators are the same,
just add or subtract the numerators!
Find the answer for each skateboard fraction problem.
Then color the skateboards.
Follow the coloring directions in the box.

1. $\frac{1}{6} + \frac{4}{6} =$ ☐

2. $\frac{9}{10} - \frac{6}{10} =$ ☐

3. $\frac{1}{3} + \frac{1}{3} =$ ☐

4. $\frac{1}{8} + \frac{1}{8} =$ ☐

5. $\frac{3}{4} + \frac{1}{4} =$ ☐

6. $\frac{2}{5} + \frac{2}{5} =$ ☐

7. $\frac{5}{8} - \frac{3}{8} =$ ☐

8. $\frac{5}{5} - \frac{1}{5} =$ ☐

9. $\frac{3}{4} - \frac{2}{4} =$ ☐

10. $\frac{4}{7} - \frac{2}{7} =$ ☐

11. $\frac{1}{10} + \frac{2}{10} =$ ☐

12. $\frac{2}{6} + \frac{3}{6} =$ ☐

Look for the answer. Then color or decorate the skateboard as the chart says.

$\frac{2}{8}$	purple
$\frac{3}{10}$	green
$\frac{5}{6}$	orange
$\frac{4}{5}$	yellow
$\frac{1}{4}$	silver
$\frac{2}{3}$	red
$\frac{2}{7}$	gold
$\frac{4}{4}$	blue

Name _____

Adding & Subtracting Fractions

Lunch on the Mountaintop

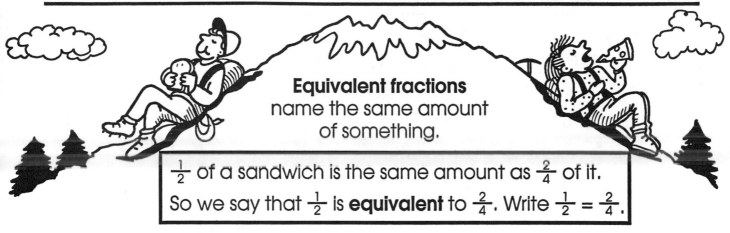

Equivalent fractions name the same amount of something.

$\frac{1}{2}$ of a sandwich is the same amount as $\frac{2}{4}$ of it.
So we say that $\frac{1}{2}$ is **equivalent** to $\frac{2}{4}$. Write $\frac{1}{2} = \frac{2}{4}$.

These mountain climbers have stopped for lunch.
Look at the food they are eating.
Write fractions that are equivalent to each other.

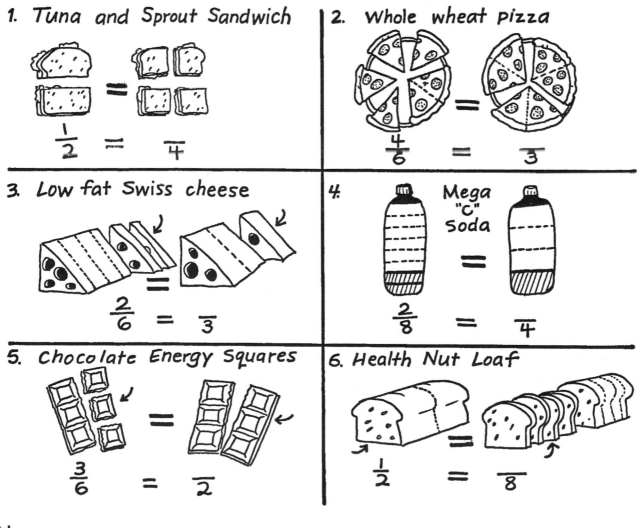

1. Tuna and Sprout Sandwich

$\frac{1}{2} = \frac{}{4}$

2. Whole wheat pizza

$\frac{4}{6} = \frac{}{3}$

3. Low fat Swiss cheese

$\frac{2}{6} = \frac{}{3}$

4. Mega "C" Soda

$\frac{2}{8} = \frac{}{4}$

5. Chocolate Energy Squares

$\frac{3}{6} = \frac{}{2}$

6. Health Nut Loaf

$\frac{1}{2} = \frac{}{8}$

Name _____

Copyright ©1998 by Incentive Publications, Inc., Nashville, TN.
Basic Skills/Math 2-3

Equivalent Fractions

Lost Skates

A **decimal** is a fraction with tenths.

You can write a decimal number as a fraction or a mixed numeral.

The decimal one-tenth (.1) is the same as the fraction $\frac{1}{10}$.

The decimal 3.5 means the same as the mixed numeral $3\frac{5}{10}$.

These skaters have each lost a skate.

Draw a line from each skater to the skate that has the matching fraction or mixed numeral. (There is an extra skate that matches no one!)

Name _____

Fractions & Decimals

Watch Out!

This scuba diver has come face-to-face with something scary under the water. What is it?

Follow the dots to find out. Connect the dots from the smallest to the largest decimal number shown.

Name _____

Ordering Decimals

A Busy Baseball Season

Nick's days get very busy during baseball season.
Here is his calendar for June.

Use the calendar to answer the questions on the next page (page 45).

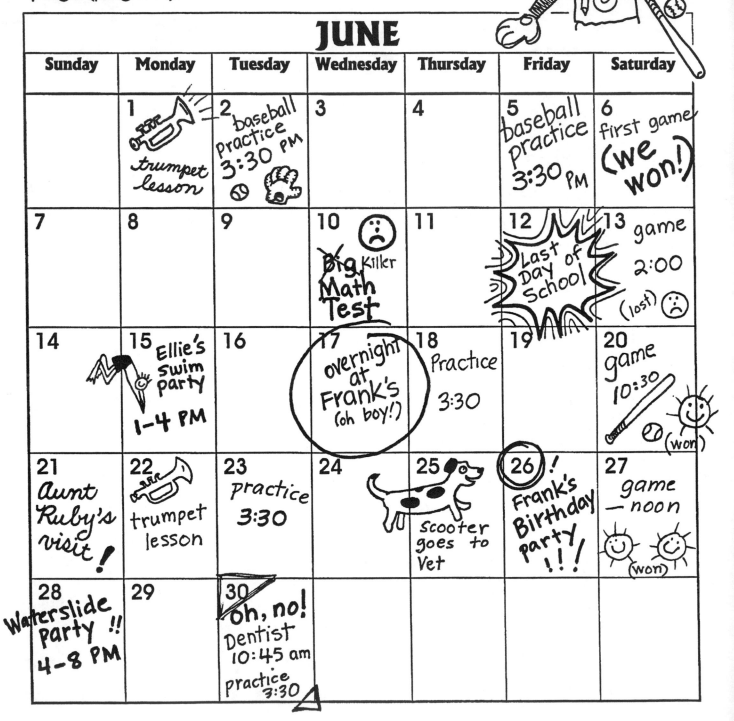

Name _____

Use with page 45.

Copyright ©1998 by Incentive Publications, Inc., Nashville, TN.
Basic Skills/Math 2-3

A Busy Baseball Season, continued . . .

1. What things does Nick have to do on June 30?

   _____ and

   _____

2. On which two dates will Nick be at Frank's?

   _____ and _____

3. How long after school gets out is Nick's dentist appointment?

   _____ weeks and _____ days

4. If Nick goes on a trip from June 18–20, what will he miss?

   _____ and

   _____

5. What is Nick looking forward to on June 15?

   _____

6. When is Aunt Ruby's visit? _____

7. What happens every Saturday in June? _____

8. Which day will he have to get Scooter into the car?

   _____

9. How many Tuesdays in June does he have practice? _____

10. How many parties will Nick go to in June? _____

11. How long is it between his trumpet lessons? _____

12. How many Mondays are there in June? _____

13. What day and date is his big math test? _____

14. How long before Frank's birthday is Ellie's party? _____

15. In which week does Nick have 2 baseball practices? _____

Name _____

Time • Calendar

Field Day Math

I'm here for the Hop, Skip, and Jump contest

FROG-EE

Field Day is an exciting day for all the kids at Walker School.

Every student needs to know the time of the events.

The schedule is posted on the fence.

Use the Field Day Schedule to solve the problems on the next page (page 47).

FIELD DAY — WALKER SCHOOL

TIME	FIELD 1	FIELD 2
9:00 A.M.	Sign-ups	Sign-ups
9:30 A.M.	3-Legged Race	Water Balloon Toss
9:45 A.M.	100 Yard Potato Sack Hop	Softball Throw
10:00 A.M.	4-Person Relay Races	Bubble Gum-Blowing Contest
11:00 A.M.		Frisbee Tournament
11:30 A.M.	Hop, Skip, & Jump	
12:00 P.M.	Lunch	Lunch
1:00 P.M.	Teacher-Kid Softball Game	Bike Rodeo
3:15 P.M.	Squirt Gun Target Shoot	Watermelon-Eating Contest
4:00 P.M.	Award Ceremony (Ribbons) and Barbecue	

Name _____

Use with page 47.

Time • Problem Solving

Copyright ©1998 by INCENTIVE PUBLICATIONS, Inc., Nashville, TN.

Basic Skills/Math 2-3

Field Day Problems

Use the Field Day Schedule on page 46.

1. Gracie gets to the field at 9:20 A.M. Does she have time to sign up for an event? _____

2. Trudy has a ballet class at 5:00 P.M. Can she compete in the watermelon-eating contest? _____

3. Chad wants to toss water balloons and be on a relay team. Which will he do first? _____

4. Name 2 events that take only 15 minutes.

   _____ and

   _____

5. Name the event that takes 1 hour.

   _____

6. Steve looks at his watch. It is 11:30 A.M. How many minutes are there until lunch? _____

7. Maggie rides to Field 2 at 1:30 P.M. What's going on when she gets there? _____

8. What time will the Frisbee™ tournament end? _____

9. What happens at the same time as the softball throw?

   _____

10. How much time is allowed for the softball game? _____

11. After lunch, Pete and Abe run home to get squirt guns. What time do they need to get back for the target shoot? _____

12. How much time does the schedule allow for relay races? _____

13. Al's friend Margie wants him to run the 3-legged race with her. He gets to Field 1 at 9:40 A.M. Is he early, late, or on time? _____

14. Erik wins a blue ribbon in the bike rodeo. What time will he go to get his award? _____

Name _____

Time • Problem Solving

Sara's Sports Schedule

Sara is busy with many sports. She has to keep a schedule.
Each clock tells what time it is when Sara arrives at one of the events.
For each problem, tell if Sara is on time.

Soccer Practice	Monday 6:30 P.M.	Chess Club	Tuesday 5:15 P.M.
Ski Meet	Saturday 11:00 A.M.	Bowling Team	Thursday 1:45 P.M.
Dance Lessons	Tuesday 2:45 P.M.	Batting Cage	Thursday 4:20 P.M.
Tennis Match	Friday 4:10 P.M.	Ice Skating Practice	Thursday 4:20 P.M.

Is she on time?

1.   yes   no

2.   yes   no

3.   yes   no

4.   yes   no

5.   yes   no

6.   yes   no

7.   yes   no

8.   yes   no

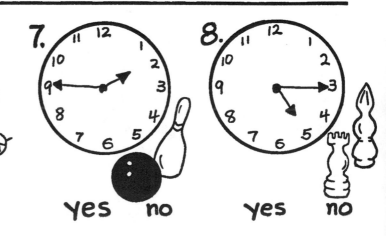

Name _____

A Pocketful of Coins

Gabe is very hungry at the soccer game.
He is buying food with the money in his pockets.
Count the coins to find how much each treat costs.

1. How much? _____

2. How much? _____

3. How much? _____

4. How much? _____

5. How much? _____

6. How much? _____

7. How much? _____

8. How much? _____

Name _____

Counting Money

Icy Problems

Hannah and Harvey can't get on the ice to play hockey until they have all the right equipment.

Here are the costs of some of the things they need for their sport.

Use this picture to help you solve the problems on the next page (page 51).

Icy Problems, continued . . .

Use the picture of the hockey players on page 50 to solve the problems.

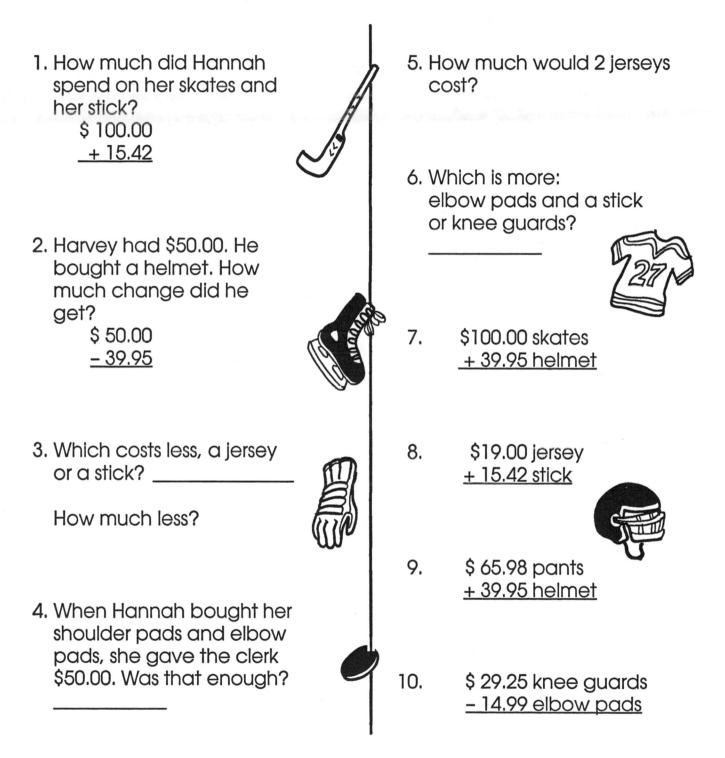

1. How much did Hannah spend on her skates and her stick?

$$\begin{array}{r} \$\,100.00 \\ +\ 15.42 \\ \hline \end{array}$$

2. Harvey had $50.00. He bought a helmet. How much change did he get?

$$\begin{array}{r} \$\,50.00 \\ -\ 39.95 \\ \hline \end{array}$$

3. Which costs less, a jersey or a stick? _____

   How much less?

4. When Hannah bought her shoulder pads and elbow pads, she gave the clerk $50.00. Was that enough?

   _____

5. How much would 2 jerseys cost?

6. Which is more: elbow pads and a stick or knee guards?

   _____

7. $$\begin{array}{r} \$\,100.00 \text{ skates} \\ +\ 39.95 \text{ helmet} \\ \hline \end{array}$$

8. $$\begin{array}{r} \$\,19.00 \text{ jersey} \\ +\ 15.42 \text{ stick} \\ \hline \end{array}$$

9. $$\begin{array}{r} \$\,65.98 \text{ pants} \\ +\ 39.95 \text{ helmet} \\ \hline \end{array}$$

10. $$\begin{array}{r} \$\,29.25 \text{ knee guards} \\ -\ 14.99 \text{ elbow pads} \\ \hline \end{array}$$

Name _____

Use with page 50.

Copyright ©1998 by Incentive Publications, Inc., Nashville, TN.
Basic Skills/Math 2-3

Problems with Money

Meet Me at the Snack Bar

During the game, Tammy and Tracy work at the snack bar.
Help them make the correct change for each customer.

MENU

ICE CREAM.........75¢
POP CORN..........25¢
FRENCH FRIES...$1.00
PIZZA..............$1.25
GUM ....10¢
SODA POP...........60¢
JUICE..............85¢
MILKSHAKE......$1.50

1. **Ice Cream**
   You give $ 1.00
   Cost   – _____
   Change

2. **Pizza**
   You give $ 2.00
   Cost   – _____
   Change

3. **2 packs of gum**
   You give   50 ¢
   Cost   – _____
   Change

4. **Juice**
   You give $ 1.00
   Cost   – _____
   Change

5. **Soda & French Fries**
   You give $ 2.00
   Cost   – _____
   Change

6. **Milkshake**
   You give $ 5.00
   Cost   – _____
   Change

7. **Popcorn**
   You give   50 ¢
   Cost   – _____
   Change

8. **French Fries**
   You give $ 5.00
   Cost   – _____
   Change

Name _____

Making Change

Basic Skills/Math 2-3

Cheers for the Team

Every team needs fans! Sports wouldn't be as much fun without them. Solve these problems about the fans at the Championship Swim Meet.

1. 35 fans were cheering for the Dolphins. 46 fans cheered for the Sharks. How many fans were cheering?

2. Carlos went to buy a snow cone from the snack bar. It cost 40¢. He had 25¢. How much more does he need?

3. Anna's mom brought hats for all 7 people in their family. Anna and Danna dropped theirs under the bleachers. How many hats were left?

4. The pool has 4 rows of bleachers with 12 spaces in each row. How many fans can fit in the bleachers?

5. Lily watched the swimmers line up for the relay. There were 5 teams, each with 4 swimmers. How many swimmers are racing in all?

6. Angie brought jelly beans for her friends in the stands. She has 100 to share among 3 friends and herself. How many jelly beans will each girl get?

Name _____

Hula Hoop Numbers

How long can each of these kids spin the hula hoop without dropping it?

The numbers in the box show the number of spins.

Write the number to match each clue next to the hoop.

0	409	254	156	621
43	311	80	7	4010

Jan
Odd number with 3 digits and a 3

June
a number = 400 + 200 − 600

Julie
a number = 106 + 100 − 50

Jamie
Even number > 78 and < 82

James
a number that has 6 in the hundreds place

Janet
> 400 with a 0 in the tens place

Jerri
a 1-digit number that is not found in any other hula hoops

Jenny
a number = 200 + 54

John
8 more than 7 x 5

Justin
2 places have 0

Name _____

Problem Solving

Basic Skills/Math 2-3

Math Words to Know

addend—a number added to another number. In the number sentence *3 + 2 = 5, 3* and *2* are addends.

decimal—a number that uses a decimal point to show tenths and hundredths, such as *.2* or *.02.*

decimal point—the dot in a decimal number.

denominator—the bottom number in a fraction. It tells how many in all. In the fraction $\frac{4}{5}$, *5* is the denominator.

difference—the answer in subtraction.

digit—the symbol *0, 1, 2, 3, 4, 5, 6, 7, 8,* or *9.*

equivalent fraction—fractions that have the same value. $\frac{2}{6}$ and $\frac{1}{3}$ are equivalent fractions.

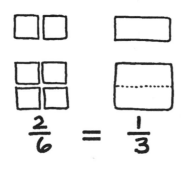

$$\frac{2}{6} = \frac{1}{3}$$

estimate—an answer that is not exact.

even number—a number that has *0, 2, 4, 6,* or *8* in the ones place.

fact family—a group of facts with the same numbers, such as: *2 + 4 = 6, 4 + 2 = 6, 6 – 2 = 4, 6 – 4 = 2.*

factor—a number that is multiplied by another number. In the number sentence *3 x 4 = 12, 3* and *4* are factors.

fraction—a number such as $\frac{1}{2}$, $\frac{3}{4}$, or $\frac{2}{3}$.

$$\frac{1}{2} \qquad \frac{3}{4} \qquad \frac{2}{3}$$

mixed number—a whole number plus a fraction, such as $1\frac{1}{2}$.

number line—a line along which numbers can be pictured. Example:

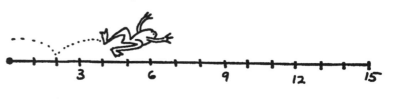

Math Words to Know

number sentence—a sentence that shows how numbers are related.
5 + 4 = 9 is a number sentence.

numerator—the top number in a fraction. It tells how many parts of the whole thing you're talking about.
In the fraction $\frac{2}{3}$, *2* is the numerator.

odd number—a number that has *1, 3, 5, 7,* or *9* in the ones place.
5, 767, 33, and *91* are odd numbers.

place value—the value a digit has in a number, such as one, ten, hundred, thousand, or ten thousand.
In the number *437, 4* is in the hundreds place, so it has a value of four hundred.

product—the answer in multiplication.
In the number sentence *6 x 7 = 42,* the product is *42.*

quotient—the answer in division.
In the number sentence *50 ÷ 10 = 5,* the quotient is *5.*

remainder—the number left over when a division is complete.
The solution for *27 ÷ 5* is *5,* with a remainder of *2.*

sum—the answer in addition.
In the number sentence *4 + 9 = 13,* the sum is *13.*

zero—the word name for the digit *0,* which means none.

Basic Skills/Math 2-3

Math Skills Test

1. Circle all the odd numbers.

    3   5   2   30   16   31

2. Circle all the even numbers.

    7   21   10   100   14   47

Write the answers.

_____ 3. In the number 473, which number is in the tens place?

_____ 4. In the number 115, which number is in the ones place?

_____ 5. In the number 716, which number is in the hundreds place?

_____ 6. In the number 2816, which number is in the hundreds place?

_____ 7. Round 56 to the nearest ten.

_____ 8. Round 73 to the nearest ten.

_____ 9. Round 228 to the nearest ten.

_____ 10. Round 472 to the nearest hundred.

11. What number sentence matches the picture? Circle the answer.

    A. 3 + 5 = 8   B. 3 x 5 = 15

12. What number sentence matches the picture? Circle the answer.

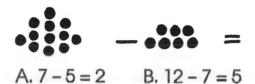

    A. 7 − 5 = 2   B. 12 − 7 = 5

13. What number sentence matches the picture? Circle the answer.

    A. 4 + 9 = 13   B. 4 x 9 = 36

Write the missing numbers in the number sentences.

14. 5 + 7 = _____

15. 3 + _____ = 7

16. 6 + 9 = _____

17. 5 + _____ = 12

18. 18 − 9 = _____

19. _____ − 6 = 5

20. 17 − _____ = 9

21. 13 − 6 = _____

22. 15 − _____ = 6

Name _____

Math Skills Test

23. What does this picture show?
Circle the answer.

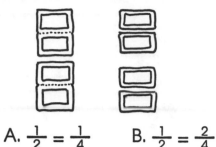

A. $\frac{1}{2} = \frac{1}{4}$ B. $\frac{1}{2} = \frac{2}{4}$

24. What does this picture show?
Circle the answer.

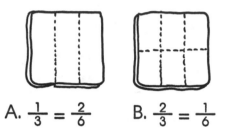

A. $\frac{1}{3} = \frac{2}{6}$ B. $\frac{2}{3} = \frac{1}{6}$

Solve the problems.

25. 403   26. 6911   27. 295
    + 192   + 1044   - 62

_____ 28. Write a fraction
that tells what
part is checkered.

_____ 29. Write a fraction
that tells what
part is checkered.

_____ 30. Write a fraction
that tells what
part is striped.

_____ 31. Write a fraction
that tells what
part has flowers.

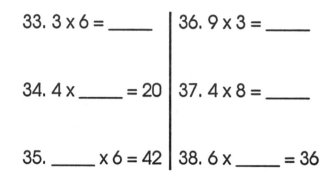

_____ 32. Write a fraction that tells
what part is checkered.

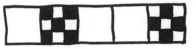

Write the missing numbers in the number sentences.

33. $3 \times 6 =$ _____ | 36. $9 \times 3 =$ _____

34. $4 \times$ _____ $= 20$ | 37. $4 \times 8 =$ _____

35. _____ $\times 6 = 42$ | 38. $6 \times$ _____ $= 36$

_____¢ 39. Count the coins. Write how
much money is shown.

_____¢ 40. Count the coins. Write how
much money is shown.

Name _____

41. Circle the number that is the largest.

111   101   10   110

42. Circle the number that is the largest.

4.5   4   1.4

Solve the problems.

43.   17
        29
     + 12

44.   101
        75
     + 11

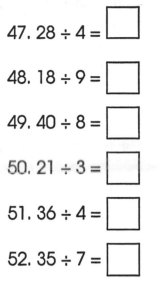

SOCCER SCORES	
TEAM	GOALS
Grizzlies	7
Eagles	2
Lions	5
Panthers	9
Cougars	6

45. Which team has the lowest score?
    A. Cougars
    B. Eagles
    C. Lions

46. Which team scored more than the Grizzlies?
    A. Lions
    B. Cougars
    C. Panthers

Write in the missing numbers in the number sentences.

47. $28 \div 4 = \Box$

48. $18 \div 9 = \Box$

49. $40 \div 8 = \Box$

50. $21 \div 3 = \Box$

51. $36 \div 4 = \Box$

52. $35 \div 7 = \Box$

Solve the problems.

53. $ 42.66
    − 13.21
  $

54.   55¢
    − 10¢
      ¢

55. $10.00
   + 12.16
  $

56. Which mixed numeral shows how much pizza is left? Circle the answer.

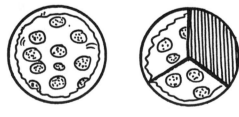

A. $1\frac{2}{3}$ B. $\frac{1}{3}$ C. $1\frac{1}{3}$

Name _____

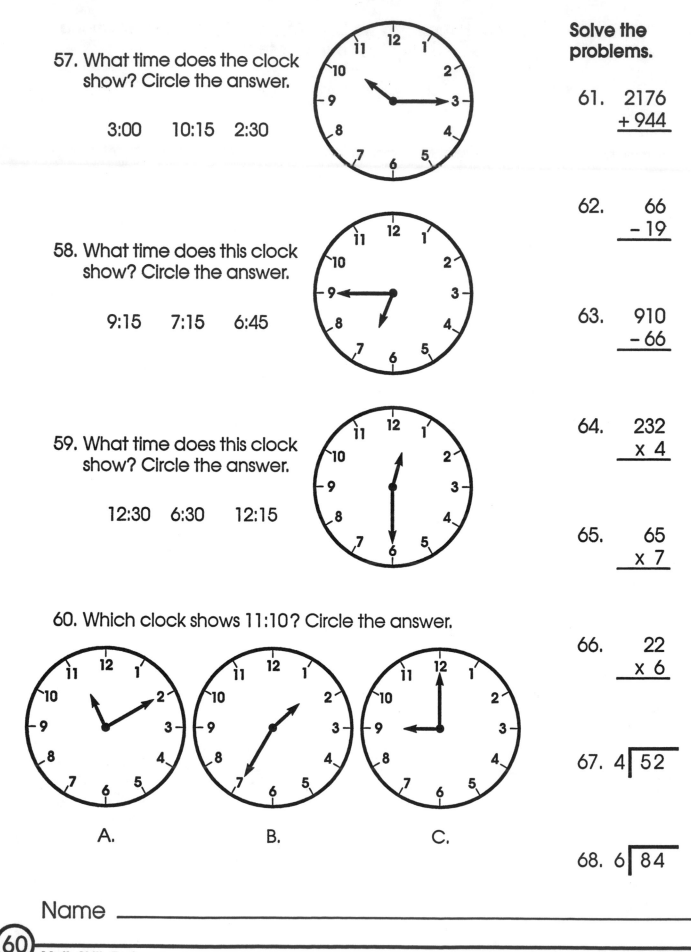

57. What time does the clock show? Circle the answer.

3:00   10:15   2:30

58. What time does this clock show? Circle the answer.

9:15   7:15   6:45

59. What time does this clock show? Circle the answer.

12:30   6:30   12:15

60. Which clock shows 11:10? Circle the answer.

A.   B.   C.

Solve the problems.

61.   2176
    + 944

62.   66
      - 19

63.   910
     - 66

64.   232
      x 4

65.   65
       x 7

66.   22
       x 6

67. 4⟌52

68. 6⟌84

Name _____

Answer Key

Skills Test

1. 3, 5, 31	24. A	45. B
2. 10, 100, 14	25. 595	46. C
	26. 7955	47. 7
3. 7	27. 233	48. 2
4. 5	28. $\frac{2}{4}$	49. 5
5. 7		50. 7
6. 8	29. $\frac{3}{5}$	51. 9
7. 60		52. 5
8. 70	30. $\frac{3}{6}$	53. $29.45
9. 230		54. 45¢
10. 500	31. $\frac{2}{8}$	55. $22.16
11. B		56. A
12. B	32. $\frac{2}{5}$	57. 10:15
13. A	33. 18	58. 6:45
14. 12	34. 5	59. 12:30
15. 4	35. 7	60. A
16. 15	36. 27	61. 3120
17. 7	37. 32	62. 47
18. 9	38. 6	63. 844
19. 11	39. 80¢	64. 928
20. 8	40. 21¢	65. 455
21. 7	41. 111	66. 132
22. 9	42. 4.5	67. 13
23. B	43. 58	68. 14
	44. 187	

Skills Exercises

page 10

A large ocean liner

page 11

Even numbers : 12, 22, 50, 66, 72, 86, 100, 444; 8 even numbers

Odd numbers: 9, 13, 27, 33, 39, 75, 103, 999, 2947; 9 odd numbers

page 12

1. George	6. eighth
2. sky diver	7. gymnastics
3. no	8. Chen
4. 18	9. seventh
5. yes	10. 81

page 13

1. 763,002	5. 24,263
2. 497	6. 9,100
3. 19,058	7. 4,907
4. 414	8. 1267

page 14

Down		Across	
1. 262	10. 421	1. 29	11. 20
2. 1000	11. 295	4. 7000	13. 22
3. 9130	12. 903	5. 211	14. 51
4. 716	13. 286	7. 30	16. 88
6. 19	15. 17	8. 96	17. 39
9. 312		9. 304	

page 15

1. 16............ pattern is x 2
2. 11, 19...... pattern is + 4
3. 7.............. pattern is – 4
4. 12............ pattern is + 1, + 2, + 3, + 4
5. 8, 5........... pattern is –1

pages 16-17

1. >	5. >	9. >	13. <
2. =	6. <	10. >	14. =
3. >	7. <	11. >	15. >
4. <	8. <	12. =	16. <

page 18

1. 1612	5. 310,923	9. 41,446
2. 15,047	6. 41,446	10. 15,047
3. 806	7. 1137	
4. 2014	8. 62,520	

page 19

1. 239	4. 422	7. 9
2. 106	5. 340	8. 110
3. 99	6. 200	9. 908

page 20

1. 30	5. 1,800	9. 5,000
2. 70	6. 900	10. 12,000
3. 690	7. 7000	
4. 600	8. 3,000	

page 21

1. 6	4. 4	7. 2
2. 7	5. 8	8. 3
3. 4	6. 4	9. 8

page 22

Hockey stick is the lost equipment.

page 23

Game 1	38	Game 7	68
Game 2	43	Game 8	46
Game 3	50 (Best)	Game 9	15
Game 4	29	Game 10	38
Game 5	50	Game 11	40
Game 6	27		

page 24

1. 92 yellow
2. 32 blue
3. 177 red
4. 35 blue
5. 86 yellow
6. 35 blue
7. 50 striped
8. 123 red
9. 49 blue
10. 76 yellow

page 25

1. 68	4. 106	7. 172	10. 22
2. 54	5. 288	8. 79	
3. 227	6. 29	9. 888	

page 26

Terry
  A. Wrong 114
  C. Wrong 120
Kerry
  E. Wrong 791

Mary
  J. Wrong 16
  L. Wrong 481
Barry
  N. Wrong 395
  O. Wrong 275

Most right? Kerry

page 27

1. 22	5. 14	9. 300	13. 400
2. 9	6. 26	10. 21	
3. 25	7. 5	11. 54	
4. 2491	8. 16	12. 4	

page 28

deer, bat, owl, bear, rabbit

page 29

Race 1
  Frannie 15
  Robbie 16
  Gus 18 Winner
Race 2
  Frannie 30 Winner
  Robbie 24
  Gus 9
Race 3
  Frannie 10
  Robbie 12 Tie
  Gus 12 Tie

Race 4
  Frannie 15 Winner
  Robbie 4
  Gus 6
Race 5
  Frannie 25 Winner
  Robbie 16
  Gus 9
Race 6
  Frannie 10
  Robbie 12 Winner
  Gus 6

page 30

1. 984	5. 2166	9. 984
2. 1336	6. 1632	10. 934
3. 1092	7. 1503	
4. 981	8. 952	

Answer: Tiger Woods

page 31

1. 8	4. 16	7. 4	10. 5
2. 9	5. 9	8. 9	11. 12
3. 27	6. 8	9. 8	12. 49

page 32

A.
  12 - 12 - 11
  9 - 13 - 9
  13 - 14 - 14
Tic Tac Toe — yes
B.
  6 - 11 - 6
  22 - 7 - 22
  12 - 4 - 12
Tic Tac Toe — yes

C.
  20 - 16 - 16
  12 - 18 - 18
  9 - 14 - 9
Tic Tac Toe — no

page 33

21 - 28 - 14 - 16 - 12 - 6 - 18 - 13 - 31
  Answer: 31

page 34

1. 4	5. 6	9. 8	13. 25
2. 2	6. 7	10. 18	14. 1
3. 7	7. 10	11. 6	15. 9
4. 5	8. 6	12. 8	16. 8

page 35

1. +	8. +	15. x
2. x	9. ÷	16. +
3. -	10. +	17. -
4. x	11. x	18. x or +
5. ÷	12. ÷	19. ÷
6. -	13. +	20. +
7. x	14. ÷	

page 36

Answers will vary.

page 37

1. E	7. D	13. F
2. C	8. B	14. B
3. F	9. M	15. M
4. H	10. G	16. L
5. B	11. J	
6. L	12. I	

page 38

1. $\frac{3}{6}$ 6. $\frac{2}{12}$

2. $\frac{5}{12}$ 7. $\frac{1}{6}$

3. $\frac{1}{6}$ 8. $\frac{4}{6}$

4. $\frac{5}{6}$ 9. $\frac{2}{6}$

5. $\frac{2}{6}$ 10. $\frac{1}{6}$

page 39

Rocky—$1\frac{1}{4}$

Ernest—$1\frac{2}{3}$

Bruiser—$2\frac{5}{6}$

Jess—$1\frac{1}{2}$

Kujo—$2\frac{3}{4}$

Bud—$1\frac{1}{6}$

Bruiser ate the most.
Bud left the most.

page 40

1. $\frac{5}{6}$—orange

2. $\frac{3}{10}$—green

3. $\frac{2}{3}$—red

4. $\frac{2}{8}$—purple

5. $\frac{4}{4}$—blue

6. $\frac{4}{5}$—yellow

7. $\frac{2}{8}$—purple

8. $\frac{4}{5}$—yellow

9. $\frac{1}{4}$—silver

10. $\frac{2}{7}$—gold

11. $\frac{3}{10}$—green

12. $\frac{5}{6}$—orange

page 41

1. $\frac{2}{4}$ 4. $\frac{1}{4}$

2. $\frac{2}{3}$ 5. $\frac{1}{2}$

3. $\frac{1}{3}$ 6. $\frac{4}{8}$

page 42

$3.3 = 3\frac{3}{10}$ (D)

$4.2 = 4\frac{2}{10}$ (I)

$.8 = \frac{8}{10}$ (A)

$6.5 = 6\frac{5}{10}$ (E)

$5.2 = 5\frac{2}{10}$ (B)

$1.1 = 1\frac{1}{10}$ (G)

$.6 = \frac{6}{10}$ (F)

$1.9 = 1\frac{9}{10}$ (C)

page 43

The picture is of a shark.

pages 44-45

1. dentist and practice
2. June 17, June 26
3. 2 weeks and 4 days
4. practice and a game
5. Ellie's swim party
6. June 21
7. a game
8. Thursday, June 25
9. 3
10. 3
11. 3 weeks
12. 5
13. Wednesday, June 10
14. 11 days
15. 1st week in June

pages 46-47

1. yes
2. yes
3. Water Balloon Toss
4. (any two) Potato Sack Hop, 3-Legged Race, Water Balloon Toss, or Softball Throw
5. Bubble Gum–Blowing Contest
6. 30 min.
7. Bike Rodeo
8. 12 P.M.
9. Potato Sack Hop
10. 2 hr. 15 min.
11. 3:15 P.M.
12. $1\frac{1}{2}$ hr.
13. late
14. 4:00 P.M.

page 48

1. no   4. yes   7. yes
2. yes   5. yes   8. yes
3. no   6. no

page 49

1. 30¢   4. 55¢   7. 20¢
2. 75¢   5. 11¢   8. 51¢
3. 60¢   6. 35¢

pages 50-51

1. $115.42
2. $10.05
3. stick; $3.58
4. yes
5. $38.00
6. elbow pads and stick
7. $139.95
8. $34.42
9. $105.93
10. $14.26

page 52

1. $ .25   5. $ .40
2. $ .75   6. $3.50
3. $ .30   7. 25¢
4. $ .15   8. $4.00

page 53

1. 81 fans
2. 15¢ more
3. 5 hats
4. 48 fans
5. 20 swimmers
6. 25 jelly beans

page 54

Jan - 311   John - 43
Jamie - 80   Julie - 156
Jerri - 7   Janet - 409
June - 0   Jenny - 254
James - 621   Justin - 4010

Answer Key